FLOORED! SUPERCARS

FORD GT

By Jared Gall

45TH PARALLEL PRESS

Published in the United States of America by Cherry Lake Publishing Group
Ann Arbor, Michigan
www.cherrylakepublishing.com

Reading Adviser: Beth Walker Gambro, MS, Ed., Reading Consultant, Yorkville, IL

Photo Credits: © Ford Images, cover, title page; © rafapress/Shutterstock, 3; © Steve Lagreca/Shutterstock, 4; © The Image Engine/Shutterstock, 6–7; Public Domain via Wikimedia Commons, 8; © The Henry Ford, 10–11; © Dan74/Shutterstock, 12–13; © Rodrigo Garrido/Shutterstock, 14; Image courtesy of Jamal Hameedi, 15; © Wirestock Creators/Shutterstock, 16; © Darren Brode/Shutterstock, 18–19; © Christopher Lyzcen/Shutterstock, 20; © tomeng/Shutterstock, 22; User:The359, CC BY-SA 3.0 via Wikimedia Commons, 23; © Andrea Bacuzzi/Dreamstime.com, 24; © The Image Engine/Shutterstock, 26; © The Image Engine/Shutterstock, 28; Valder137, CC BY 2.0 via Wikimedia Commons, 30 (top); © i viewfinder/Shutterstock, 30 (bottom); Dave Doe from Ottawa, Ontario, Canada, via Wikimedia Commons, 31 (top); © Steve Lagreca/Shutterstock, 31 (bottom)

45th Parallel Press is an imprint of Cherry Lake Publishing Group.

Library of Congress Cataloging-in-Publication Data

Names: Gall, Jared, author.
Title: Ford GT / by Jared Gall.
Description: Ann Arbor, Michigan : 45th Parallel Press, [2025] | Series: Floored! Supercars | Audience: Grades 4-6 | Summary: "Tech and innovation are at the forefront of luxury supercars. This book explores the cool features that make Ford GTs some of the best high-performance vehicles in the world. From the history of the brand, to fast facts, and awesome photos--these books have enough to keep any car enthusiast engaged. This high-interest series is written at a low readability to aid struggling readers. Books feature educational sidebars, table of contents, glossary, index, author biography, and timeline"-- Provided by publisher.
Identifiers: LCCN 2024035972 | ISBN 9781668956625 (hardcover) | ISBN 9781668957479 (paperback) | ISBN 9781668958346 (ebook) | ISBN 9781668959213 (pdf)
Subjects: LCSH: Ford GT automobile--History--Juvenile literature. | Ford GT automobile--Design and construction--Juvenile literature.
Classification: LCC TL215.F7 G35 2025 | DDC 629.222/2--dc23/eng/20240923
LC record available at https://lccn.loc.gov/2024035972

Printed in the United States of America

Note from Publisher: Websites change regularly, and their future contents are outside of our control. Supervise children when conducting any recommended online searches for extended learning opportunities.

ABOUT THE AUTHOR:

Jared Gall writes about cars and trucks for magazines and websites. He has driven everything from semitrucks and school buses to sports cars and supercars. He has raced off-road buggies through the desert in Mexico and Mercedes-Benzes on frozen lakes in Sweden. He has driven a lot of Mercedes-Benzes, but never an AMG One. His personal top speed is 189 miles (304.2 kilometers) per hour, set while driving a Ferrari.

Table of Contents

A Ford GT is a supercar. Not everyone can buy it. They start at $500,000.

CHAPTER 1

Introduction

There are many kinds of cars. They're good at different things. Minivans have lots of space. Whole families can fit. They can ride together to school. They can ride together on vacation. **Sport utility vehicles** are called SUVs. They also have lots of space. They're made to tow heavy things. They tow boats. They tow campers. They also go off-roading.

Sports cars are built to be fast. They're fun to drive. They're small. They're light. This makes them **agile**. Agile means they can turn quickly and easily. They can go around corners fast.

Supercars are like sports cars. But they go even faster. Their engines have more power. They're lighter. They go faster on straight roads. They turn faster. Many are built with special metal. This makes them extra light.

Most supercars sit low. They're close to the ground. This makes them **aerodynamic**. That means they move through air easily. Imagine putting your hand out a car window. Imagine facing your palm into the wind. It would be hard to keep your hand still. But what if you lay your hand flat? It would then be easier to hold your hand steady. Your hand is more aerodynamic when it's flat. Being aerodynamic makes supercars fast.

There aren't many Ford GT cars. They're hard to find. This makes them more special.

Henry Ford with his son Edsel Bryant Ford (left), and his 2 grandsons: Henry Ford II (middle), and William Clay (right).

CHAPTER 2

Ford GT History

Henry Ford was an American businessman. He started Ford Motor Company. Henry Ford II was his grandson. He took over in 1945. He wanted to buy the Ferrari company. Ferrari was a top carmaker. It made race cars and supercars.

Enzo Ferrari is Italian. He was the **founder** of Ferrari. Founders start something. Ferrari was going to sell his company to Ford in 1963. But he changed his mind. Henry Ford II was mad. He decided to get even. He aimed to beat Ferrari in a race.

The **24 Hours of Le Mans** is a famous race. It takes place in France. It happens once every year. It lasts for 24 hours straight. That's a whole day and night! It starts on a Saturday afternoon. It ends on Sunday afternoon.

All 3 Ford GTs had broken down by the 12-hour mark at the 1964 24 Hours of Le Mans race.

There are teams of drivers. Each team has 2 or 3 drivers. They take turns driving. They take turns eating. They take turns sleeping. Winners finish the most laps in 24 hours.

Ford designed the GT40. GT stands for **grand tourer**. Such cars can go a long distance. They go at high speeds. They're also fancy.

The GT40 was 40 inches (101.6 centimeters) tall. That's not tall for a car. For example, the Mazda Miata is a tiny sports car. It's

49 inches (124.5 cm) tall. The Ford GT was very, very low. That made it aerodynamic.

In 1963, Ford was working on the GT40. That year, Ferrari won Le Mans. The GT40 was ready in 1964. Ford entered 3 GT40s in Le Mans that year. All 3 cars broke down. Ferrari won again. Ford competed again in 1965. All the GT40s broke down again. Ferrari won again.

Ford went to work. It made the GT40 more **reliable**. Reliable means steady. Ford drivers needed to count on the GT40. They needed it not to break down.

Ford entered Le Mans in 1966. A Ford GT40 was in first place when the race was almost over. Another one was in second place. And another was in third place. The GT40 in first place slowed

down. This let the other GT40s catch up. The cars were in the last lap. All 3 cars crossed the finish line together. Henry Ford II had the win he wanted.

Ford won Le Mans again. It won the next 3 years in a row. Ford proved it could beat Ferrari. It stopped making GT40s. It didn't make another car like it for almost 40 years.

Ford had reached its goal of beating Ferrari at Le Mans. Many thought the Ford GT adventure was over, but they were wrong.

A Ford Ranger races through the desert in Teruel, Spain.

Behind the Wheel

Jamal Hameedi is an engineer. Engineers design things. They build things. Hameedi worked at Ford. He did this for more than 20 years. He helped make Ford cars faster. He improved trucks for racing off-road through the desert.

He also worked on supercars. He helped build the Ford GT. He did this in 2005. He was then put in charge of Ford's high-performance cars. He builds cars to go fast. He also makes them look good. He said, "Seeing something go from an idea to something an assembly plant makes day in and day out is extremely rewarding." Assembly plants are factories where things are made.

Concept cars *are model cars used to show off new styles. They rarely get made. But the Ford GT did.*

CHAPTER 3

Ford GT Evolution

Ford Motor Company turned 100 years old in 2003. It wanted to celebrate. It was proud of the GT40. So it made a new GT40. It was going to build only one. It would take it to auto shows. Such cars are called concept cars. Concept cars look cool. But they're not meant to be sold. They show off new styles. They show off new tech. Ford wanted to show off the new GT40. It did this at the 2002 Detroit Auto Show.

The Detroit Auto Show is very important. Every big car company goes. They come from all over the world. They see what other companies are making. Everybody loved the new GT40. Ford decided to build more. It also decided to sell them.

The new GT40 went on sale in 2005. Ford just called it the GT. That's because it was taller than the GT40. The GT engine was smaller than the GT40 engine. The new engine had a **supercharger**. This device goes on top of the engine. It forces more air into it. That helps the engine make more power.

The GT was very powerful. It could go from 0 to 60 miles (0 to 96.6 kilometers) per hour. It could do this in less than 4

seconds. A normal car needs about 8 seconds to do that. And the GT could go more than 200 miles (321.9 km) per hour. The fastest cars can go on most U.S. highways is 70 miles (112.7 km) per hour.

Ford built this GT for just 2 years. It did this in 2005 and 2006. It never raced it. But lots of owners did.

The new GT had special doors. The doors rolled up into the roof. This made it easier to get in and out.

A 2006 GT can be painted like the original Le Mans race cars.

Some owners compete in the Texas Mile race. It's in Texas. Cars go one at a time. They start standing still. Then they go as fast as they can. They race for a single mile.

Some owners **modify** their cars. Modify means to change. It means to improve. A modified Ford GT holds the record at the Texas Mile. It went 300 miles (482.8 km) per hour. That's faster than many airplanes fly!

Fast Facts

- Bruce McLaren drove the GT40. He raced at Le Mans. He did this in 1966. He started his own car company. McLaren's company still makes supercars today.
- Ford built 5 GT40s with no roofs. They were called the X-1. Four of them still exist. One of them sold for almost $7 million. This happened in 2017.
- Cameras were mounted to a GT40. They were used to record video of the 1970 Le Mans race. This was for a movie about the race. Porsche was another camera car. It actually took part in the race. It finished ninth.
- Somebody bought one of the GT40s from the Le Mans movie. The car sold for $11 million. This happened in 2012. It was the most expensive GT40 ever.

There are vents on the hood of the Ford GT. These help with airflow. They make the aerodynamics better.

Ford went to a different auto show in 2005. It showed off another GT concept car. This one was a **convertible** version. Convertibles are special cars. Their roofs fold down. Ford's new car was called the GTX1. Everyone loved it. Ford decided to sell it to customers.

Ford hired a different company to build the GTX1. That company started with finished GTs. Then it cut off the roof. It made new doors. It made new engine covers. It was a lot of extra work. That made the GTX1 more costly. The GTX1 is very rare. Ford built only 38 of them.

It cost $38,000 to cut the roof off each GT. That's as much as many cars cost.

Ford won Le Mans in 2016. The company was the top in its class.

CHAPTER 4

Ford GT Today

It was the early 2010s. Ford's first Le Mans win was in 1966. Then 2016 marked 50 years after this win. Ford wanted to race again. It aimed to race in 2016. It had stopped building the GT 10 years before. It decided to make a new one.

This GT was special. It was the first to be built for racing and for the road. Race cars are different from street cars. Race cars only have to be fast. Cars for the street need to be comfortable. They need to be safe. They need to be **efficient**. Efficient means not wasting energy. Efficient cars can drive farther without stopping for gas. But the Ford GT is both a race car and a street car.

Most cars are made from steel or aluminum. The GT is made from **carbon fiber**. Carbon fiber is very light. It's very strong. Race cars can go fast if they're light. Carbon fiber is costly. Normal cars aren't made from carbon fiber.

Ford wanted the new GT to be super aerodynamic. There's a button on the **dashboard**. Dashboards are information displays. Drivers can push this button. That lowers the GT. This lets it cut through the air more easily. But it also makes the ride bumpy. It's harder to drive. Ford calls this "track mode." It means car bottoms are very close to the ground. It makes driving over speed bumps hard.

Even the Ford GT's wheels are carbon fiber. Ford was the first to make carbon fiber wheels.

Cost of Ownership

MODEL	PRICE
2024 Toyota Camry	$27,500
2024 Honda CR-V	$31,000
2024 Ford F-150	$39,000

MODEL	PRICE
2017 Ford GT	$454,000
2020 Ford GT Mk II	$1,200,000
2023 Ford GT Mk IV	$1,700,000

The Ford GT has a wing on its back. When it's not driving fast, the wing lays flat. The wing pops up when the car is going fast. This makes **downforce.** Downforce is when air pushes something against the ground.

Imagine putting your hand out the car window again. When your hand is flat, it's easy to keep still. Now imagine tilting your hand down toward the ground. The wind will push your hand down. That is downforce. On a race car, downforce pushes the car against the track. That helps it go around turns faster.

Everything matters on supercars. Every curve, vent, and wing matters. They help create speed.

The GT is Ford's most expensive car. It cost $454,000 to make. It's also Ford's fastest car. It can go 216 miles (347.6 km) per hour. Ford also made 2 special edition GTs. One was called the Mk II (Mark 2). The other one was the Mk IV (Mark 4). They're more powerful than the GT. Neither one was **street legal**. Street legal means driving on public roads. GT owners can't drive them on regular roads. The cars are too fast! They can be driven only on racetracks.

Ford stopped building the GT in 2023. Do you think it'll make another one someday?

Timeline of a Legend

1963
- Enzo Ferrari refuses to sell his company to Henry Ford II. This upsets Ford.

1966
- Ford races the GT40 at Le Mans. The company takes first, second, and third places.

1970
- Ford stops making the GT40.

2002
- Ford shows off t
GT concept car.

2005
- Second-generatio
Ford GT goes on

2006

Ford stops making the GT.

2016

Ford GT wins Le Mans.

2017

Third-generation Ford GT is produced.

2022

Ford stops making the street-legal GT.

2023

GT Mk IV is the last GT built.

Find Out More

BOOKS

Duling, Kaitlyn. *Ford GT.* Minneapolis, MN: Bellwether Media, 2023.

Labrecque, Ellen. *Ford GT.* Minneapolis, MN: Kaleidoscope, 2020.

WEBSITES

Search these online sources with an adult:

Ford GT40 Origins | Ford Corporate

Ford GT Supercar | Ford

Glossary

24 Hours of Le Mans (twen-tee-FOHR OW-uhrz uhv luh MAHNZ) a famous endurance race in France

aerodynamic (air-oh-dye-NAA-mik) able to move easily through the air

agile (A-juhl) able to change direction quickly

carbon fiber (KAR-buhn FYE-buhr) a very strong, lightweight material

concept cars (KAHN-sept KARZ) cars built for auto shows but generally not sold to the public

convertible (kuhn-VUHR-tuh-buhl) a car with a top that can be lowered or removed

dashboard (DASH-bord) instruments, controls, and information displays in a car

downforce (DOWN-fors) a downward aerodynamic force

efficient (IH-fih-shuhnt) able to be more productive with less energy

founder (FOWN-duhr) a person who starts something

grand tourer (GRAND TOOR-uhr) a car designed to drive at high speed for long distances; also called GT

modify (MAH-duh-fye) to change or improve

reliable (rih-LYE-uh-buhl) dependable

sport utility vehicles (SPORT yoo-TIH-luh-tee VEE-uh-kuhlz) vehicles designed to be used on rough surfaces but often used on city streets; also called SUVs

street legal (STREET LEE-guhl) allowed to be driven on public roads

supercars (SOO-puhr-kahrz) cars designed to go faster than other cars

supercharger (SOO-puhr-char-juhr) a device that forces more air into the engine and helps the engine make more power

Index